ring

bague

sheep

mouton

rain

pluie

doctor

médecin

morning  Matin	breakfast  petit déjeuner
duck  canard	ladybug  coccinelle

| win  gagner | school  école |
| farmer  agriculteur | zipper  fermeture éclair |

gift  cadeau	singing  en chantant
whale  baleine	jam  confiture

squirrel  écureuil	mother  mère
king  Roi	jump  saut

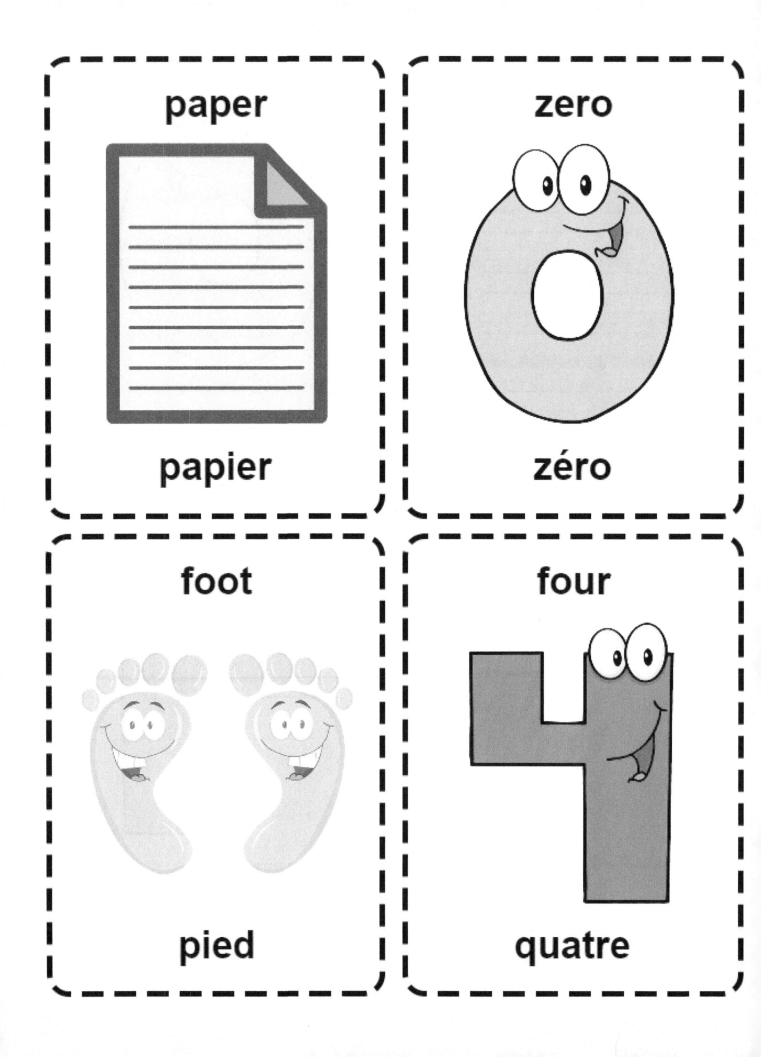

toothbrush 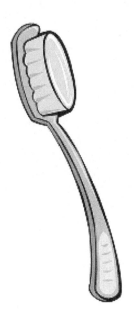 **brosse à dents**	**volcano**  **volcan**
hug  **étreinte**	**brother**  **frère**

goodbye Au revoir	**apple** Pomme
earth Terre	**boat** bateau

wake up	bicycle

Réveillez-vous	vélo
ant	sister

fourmi	sœur

eight huit	**worm** ver
alligator alligator	**girl** fille

icecream  crème glacée	violin  violon
playground  Cour de récréation	wind  vent

pig  porc	deer  cerf
yogurt  yaourt	teach  Enseigner

elephant	laugh

l'éléphant	rire
ironing	sick

repassage	malade

eat	plane
manger	avion |//
watermelon	bed
pastèque	lit

question	ballon

question	ballon

chair	clean
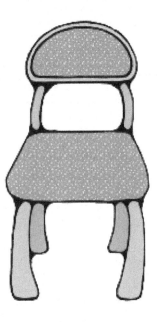	
chaise	nettoyer

swimming	nine

nager	neuf
bird's nest	corn

le nid d'oiseau	blé

drum	hurt

tambour	blesser
octopus	snake

poulpe	serpent

book livre	**fish** poisson
chicken poulet	**umbrella** parapluie

doll

poupée

drink

boisson

snail

escargot

read

lis

bedroom	shower

chambre	douche

bread	box

pain	boîte

run  courir	bus  autobus
cry  cri	fall  tomber

hedgehog  hérisson	medicine  médicament
shoe  chaussure	hand  main

vase	gun

vase	pistolet

love	milk

amour	Lait

toilet toilette	**play**  jouer
train 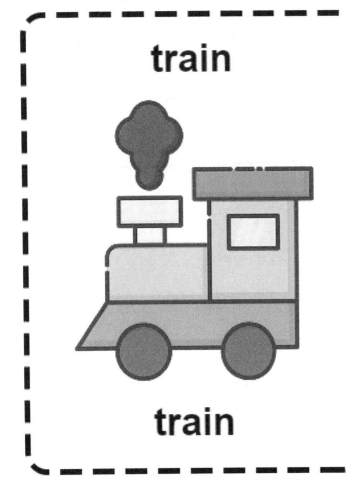 train	**friend**  ami

night	sleeping

nuit	en train de dormir
lion	car

Lion	voiture

comb  peigne	children  les enfants
zebra  zèbre	strawberry  fraise

suitcase	unicorn

valise	Licorne

math	xylophone

math	xylophone

window	home

la fenêtre	maison

jet	eye

jet	œil

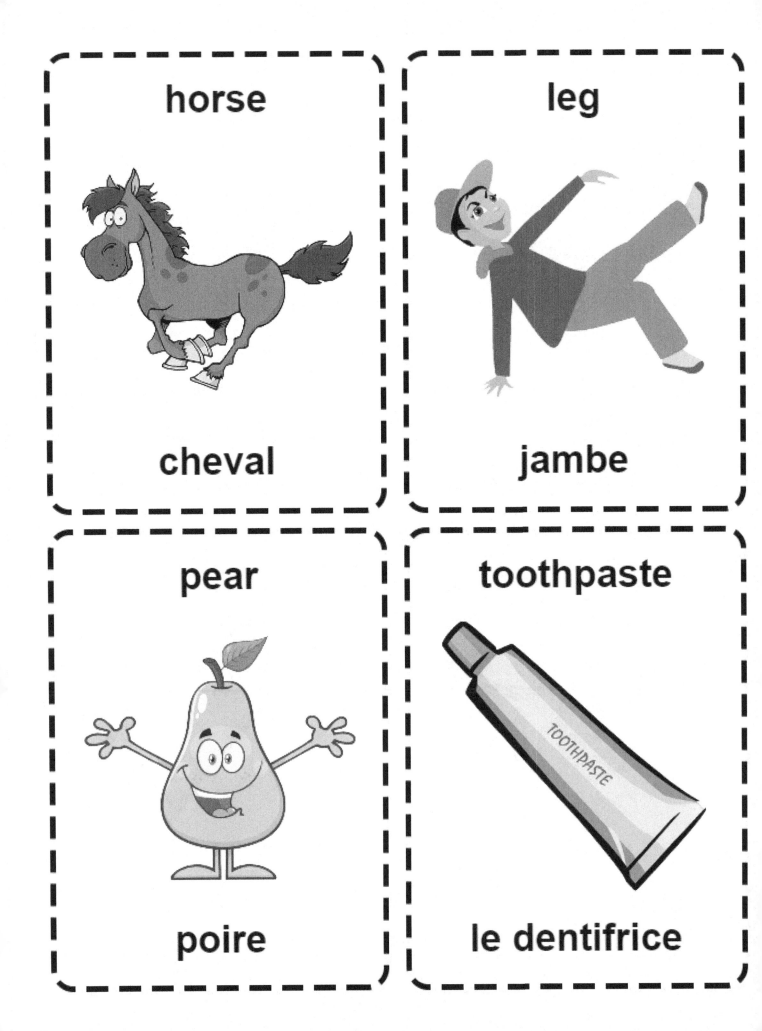

homework	bag

devoirs	sac

piano	wash
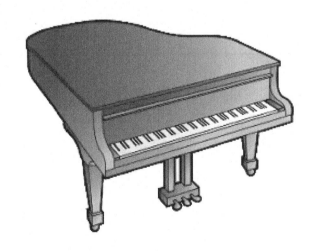	
piano	lavage

turkey	pineapple

dinde	ananas

giraffe	truck

girafe	un camion

flower	shark

fleur	requin

sad	baseball

triste	base-ball

man	writing

homme	l'écriture

door	bee

porte	abeille

groundhog  marmotte	queen  reine
working  travail	tiger  tigre

socks
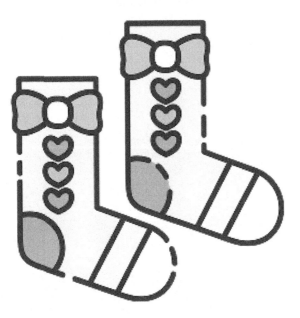
chaussettes

moon

lune

hair

cheveux

soccer

football

birthday

anniversaire

ram

RAM

bone

os

water

eau

happy

heureux

climbing

escalade

yarn

fil

kangaroo

kangourou

cooking	cake
cuisine	gâteau

ball	cow
ballon	vache

two deux	van van
baby bébé	presents présente

drawing

dessin

shopping

achats

father

père

one

un

Made in the
USA
Middletown, DE

74877239R00064